COLLECTAFACT ™

ANCIENT GREECE

TWO CAN ™

PRINCETON ■ LONDON

What's in this book

*All words in the text which appear in **bold** can be found in the glossary*

3

ITALY

Adriatic Sea

Pindus Mountains

MACEDONIA

TROY

Aegean Sea

Delphi

Athens

Peloponnese

Ionian Sea

Olympia

Sparta

Sea of Crete

CRETE
Home of
the Minotaur

The Greek world

The civilization of ancient Greece began
around 2000 B.C. The Greeks controlled the
mainland and the islands we now know as
Greece. As the civilization expanded, traders
and farmers settled in the lands at the
eastern end of the Mediterranean Sea.

The peak of the Greek civilization was
known as the **Classical period**, between
479 B.C. and 323 B.C. During this time, the
Greeks developed many new ideas about
science and the arts. Some of their ideas
and inventions influenced other civilizations
in Europe at that time. From there, Greek
ideas spread all around the world.

ASIA MINOR

Land conquered by
Alexander the Great

RHODES

CYPRUS

The Greeks traveled
to these areas to farm
the land.

Mediterranean Sea

FastFact
One of the
ancient battle
tactics was to
row very fast
toward a ship
and ram into the side of it!

Alexandria

EGYPT

Land and climate

Mainland Greece and the nearby islands are hot and dry with high mountains and steep-sided valleys. The mainland is surrounded almost entirely by water. It was once covered in forest but by the **Classical period**, many trees had been cut down. The scarce farmland was located mainly near the coast or in sheltered valleys.

The most important crops were wheat, barley, grapes, and olives. The Greeks were skilled sailors and keen traders and they imported a lot of their food from other countries. There were few good roads and most journeys had to be made on foot. Some village communities were very isolated.

▼ Because traveling overland was so difficult, the Greeks often traveled by sea. They found their way by staying close to the coasts. The sea was often stormy and sometimes there were attacks by pirates.

▶ This picture shows some olive trees growing on a dry, rocky hillside.

The five ages of ancient Greece

People have been living in the lands of Greece for over 40,000 years! The early Greek people lived in caves. Instead of farming their food, they hunted animals and gathered plants to eat.

Around 6500 B.C., the Greek way of life was just beginning. Small groups of people lived on the islands in the Aegean Sea and the Sea of Crete. The people in this region grew crops, kept sheep, and made clay pots. Most of their tools and weapons were made from stone.

In the strong and influential ancient Greek civilization that grew from these groups of people, there were five major periods of time.

The Bronze Age: 3000–1000 B.C.

The Bronze Age was when the Greeks began to use **bronze** to make their crafts, tools, and weapons. Around 1900 B.C. there were two main groups of people living in ancient Greece. The Minoans lived on the island of Crete, and the Myceneans lived on the mainland of Greece.

In 1500 B.C., a huge volcano erupted near Crete and many Minoan people were killed. Soon after, their capital city, Knossos, burned down and was never rebuilt. In 1250 B.C., the Trojan War began. It lasted ten years.

The Dark Age: 1000–800 B.C.

The ancient Greeks have kept us in the dark about this period! There are no written records from this time because in the Dark Age hardly anyone knew how to read and write. Instead, people kept their legends alive through traditional songs and stories.

We do know that the population of Greece became smaller around this time. By the time of the Dark Age in ancient Greece, the powerful Egyptian civilization had come to an end. In China, the Shang dynasty was also ending.

The Archaic period: 800–479 B.C.

During the Archaic period, the Greek civilization began to spread to other lands around the Mediterranean Sea, and the **city-states** began to form.

Until about 800 B.C., the Greeks had not used writing for hundreds of years. During the Archaic period, the Greeks began to write again. **Homer** is thought to have composed his two famous poems about the Trojan War around this time, *The Iliad* and *The Odyssey*.

In 776 B.C. the first ever Olympic Games were held at Olympia.

The Classical period: 479–323 B.C.

The ancient Greek civilization reached its peak during the **Classical period**. Part of this period, from about 477 B.C. onward, is known as the Golden Age. The arts, such as plays, stories, **sculpture**, and architecture flourished. The discoveries and teachings of the **philosophers** of this time continue to influence people today.

In 431 B.C. the Peloponnesian war broke out between Athens and Sparta. After 27 years, Athens was conquered. In 338 B.C. Greece was defeated in a war against Macedonia and by 323 B.C. Greek independence had ended.

The Hellenistic Age: 323–31 B.C.

In 323 B.C. **Alexander the Great** died. The period after his death is known as the Hellenistic Age. For the next 150 years, Greece was ruled by the Macedonians.

During the Hellenistic Age, another **empire** was growing not far away. By 272 B.C., the Romans had conquered most of Italy. Around 146 B.C., the Romans conquered Greece and Macedonia. The Roman Empire was large and powerful but this did not destroy the Greek way of life. In fact, many Greek traditions became part of the Roman way of life.

The city-states

Greece was not always the united country that it is today. It was once made up of separate **city-states**. Each city-state was based around one city and included the surrounding farms and villages.

Athens was one of the largest and most powerful city-states. At the height of the **Classical period**, there were more than 250,000 people living in the city and the surrounding countryside. Artists, **philosophers**, and politicians from Athens were famous throughout Greece.

▼ This is the ancient city of Athens. On a hill, called the Acropolis, was the Parthenon, the main temple of the city. In the center of town was the busy agora where markets took place.

FastFact
The ancient Greek tradition of the Olympic Games was banned in 393 A.D. by a Roman emperor. But it began again in 1896 and continues today.

Athens versus Sparta

Sparta was Athens' main rival. There were many wars between the two cities as they both tried to gain control of Greece. Sparta was famed for the strength of its army. In 431 B.C. the rivalry between the two cities led to the Peloponnesian War. After 27 years of fighting, Sparta won the war.

▲ This vase painting shows some Greek soldiers in battle.

▶ Ancient Greek soldiers used weapons and armor made from iron or bronze.

A divided Greece

Life was not always peaceful in ancient Greece. The people lived in many different **city-states**. Some of these were friends but others were enemies.

Over the course of hundreds of years, there were many wars between the city-states. There were also independent territories, which did not get involved in the fighting at all, and some pirates.

The two worst enemies were Sparta and Athens. By 500 B.C., they were the most powerful city-states and they each had many **allies**.

Corinth

Corinth helped to start the Peloponnesian War. In 431 B.C., Corinth had a disagreement with Corcyra. Corcyra is an island to the west of Greece, in the Ionian Sea. Today, it is called Corfu. The disagreement escalated into a battle and the two biggest city-states, Sparta and Athens, had to step in with extra troops. Sparta backed Corinth while Athens supported Corcyra. This led to the Peloponnesian war.

The Spartan allies

Sparta had the finest army of all the city-states. To the Spartans, war was the most important part of life. All Spartan men were expected to join the army. Boys trained as soldiers when they were only seven years old! Sparta and Athens both wanted to control Greece. The Peloponnesian war between Athens and Sparta started in 431 B.C. Sparta eventually defeated Athens after 27 years of fighting and ruled over Greece. But the Spartans were not as good at ruling as they were at fighting. They only stayed in power for about 30 years before they were defeated by the Thebans.

The Thebans

The warriors of Thebes were the most hated in Greece. This was probably because they were always changing their mind about which side they were on! First the Thebans joined the Persians. Then they became allies with Sparta but later turned against them. And the next time there was a war against the Persians, the Thebans stayed on the Greek side! Eventually, Thebes was destroyed by **Alexander the Great**'s armies.

The Persian Empire

In 550 B.C., the Persian **Empire** began to expand and soon ruled over parts of Asia Minor and Egypt. The Persians conquered the Greek territories in the west of Asia Minor. In 499 B.C., the Greeks rebelled, and over the next 20 years they won a series of wars against the Persians. In 359 B.C., Philip II became king of Macedonia. His armies were strong and in 338 B.C. Greece fell under Macedonian control. Two years later, Philip died and his son Alexander became king. Alexander was a brilliant soldier and in 324 B.C. with an army of 35,000 men, he conquered the whole Persian Empire.

Olympia
In the month before the Olympic Games began, all wars between the city-states ceased so that people could travel safely to the games. Olympia was one of Sparta's allies.

Crete
The island of Crete was an independent territory. The people of the island traded and communicated with the Greeks, but they did not become involved in the quarrels between the city-states. The pirates of Crete were feared throughout Greece!

MACEDONIA

Delphi

Thebes

Marathon

Athens

Corinth

Sparta

PERSIAN EMPIRE

Ephesus
Ephesus was one of the Greek city-states on the west coast of Asia Minor. A huge **temple** was built here to worship the goddess Artemis, the goddess of women and fertility. During the **Classical period**, the city-states in this region fought many battles against the Persian Empire.

KEY
- Spartan Allies
- Athenian Allies
- Independent Territories

The Athenian allies

Athens was the greatest of the city-states. It was here that the ancient Greek civilization reached its peak. The Athenians were successful in battle, too. They had a large fleet of ships, called **triremes**, and many allies around the Aegean Sea. But on land, the Athenian army was not so strong.

Unlike many other city-states, Athens did not have a permanent army. Instead, all men between the ages of 20 and 50 were on call to go into battle when war broke out. They suffered heavily in some of the land-based battles against enemies such as Sparta and Macedonia.

Power of the people

In ancient Greece, some groups of people had different rights from others. **Citizens** were the most important group of people and they had the most rights. They could own property and take part in **politics**. Only adult men were allowed to be citizens in ancient Greece.

   Slaves were the property of their owners and they had no rights at all. Many slaves lived in miserable conditions. But some slaves were paid for the work they did and if they saved enough money they could buy their freedom.

▲ These are some ancient Greek coins.

▼ Soldiers often watched over slaves as they worked.

FastFact
In the late nineteenth century, the remains of the original games' stadium at Olympia were found. In 1896, the first modern Olympics were held in Athens.

▲ Women could not vote, and were not allowed to do things on their own. They had lots of housework to do, like the women collecting water on this vase.

Government

In many of the **city-states** in ancient Greece, the government was run as a **democracy**. All of the decisions about the city-state were made by councils of citizens. Other city-states, however, were ruled by rich and powerful landowners.

In Athens, all citizens could vote to decide on issues such as the type of taxes to be paid and whether or not to go to war. All citizens could take part in politics and legal affairs. Some citizens were paid a full day's wages to attend the government assemblies.

▲ Discs such as these were used to vote in courts of law. Hollow discs stood for "guilty" and solid discs stood for "not guilty."

▲ Citizens could vote against a politician by writing his name on a pottery fragment, called an ostrakon.

Philosophy and science

The ancient Greeks were curious about themselves and the world around them. They made many important advances in science, learning, and the arts. Great thinkers were known as **philosophers** regardless of what subject they studied. The word philosopher comes from the Greek words for "lover of wisdom." Philosophers tried to find out how the universe worked and how people should best live their lives.

Many Greek discoveries provide the foundations of our knowledge and beliefs.

The Greeks studied the stars and learned that Earth floats freely in space and turns on an imaginary line called an axis. They also correctly predicted eclipses of the sun. But sometimes the Greeks were wrong. One scholar named Ptolemy thought that Earth was the center of the universe.

Few of the Greeks' ideas were used for solving practical problems. For example, they did not use their metal-working techniques to make tools that would increase their knowledge of science.

Famous philosophers

● **Socrates (about 469–399 B.C.)**
Socrates was one of the first great philosophers of Classical Greece. He questioned many of the beliefs of the time.

● **Hippocrates (about 469–399 B.C.)**
Hippocrates was alive at the same time as Socrates. He practiced scientific medicine and studied the human body.

● **Plato (about 429–347 B.C.)**
Plato founded a school in Athens called The Academy where he taught Aristotle.

● **Aristotle (about 384–322 B.C.)**
Aristotle examined things in nature and developed a way of thinking called logic.

▲ A bust of Socrates.

◀ The philosopher Eratosthenes used the sun to calculate the circumference of the Earth. At noon, the sun was directly overhead in Syene in Southern Egypt. So, he measured the angle of the sun at Alexandria, in Northern Egypt, and then measured the distance between the two places. His calculation of the Earth's circumference was off by just 200 miles (320km).

FastFact
In Spartan schools, boys were taught to be tough. They had to sleep on the ground and were beaten if they misbehaved.

Gods and goddesses

The Greeks worshipped many gods and goddesses that represented parts of human life or the natural world. The gods were thought to live on **Mount Olympus** and there were many stories about them in which they fought among each other or fell in love, just like human beings.

There were many **temples** where **priests** or **priestesses** performed rituals in honor of the gods. Offerings of food and wine were made and sometimes during **festivals** **sacrifices** were made.

The Greeks believed that the gods controlled events. So they looked to the gods for answers to their problems. Some problems were solved by a **soothsayer** who studied the weather or the remains of animals for answers from the gods. Other problems required a visit to an **oracle** where a priest or priestess passed on messages from the gods.

▼ At the oracle in Delphi, a priestess called the Pythia, went into a trance to receive messages from the gods.

The Olympic Games

In ancient Greece, games and festivals were held to honor the gods. The Olympic Games were held in Olympia in honor of Zeus every four years. They lasted for five days and the events included boxing, wrestling, running, long jump, discus throwing, javelin throwing, and chariot races. People came from all over Greece to compete in the games. All wars were postponed so that people could travel safely to see them.

Important gods

Zeus was the king of the gods.
Hera was married to Zeus and was the queen of the gods.
Poseidon was the god of the sea.
Demeter was the goddess of growing food.
Ares was the god of war.
Hermes was the messenger of the gods.
Apollo was the god of music and healing.

▲ Aphrodite, the goddess of love.

◄ Athena, the goddess of wisdom, was born from the head of Zeus.

Theater and writing

The ancient Greeks were one of the first groups of people to record their **history** as it happened. Before this, people had passed on information by word of mouth.

Poetry was the earliest form of Greek literature. Many of the Greek poems told stories about heroes and gods. **Homer** was an ancient storyteller. He composed two **epic** poems called *The Iliad* and *The Odyssey*. These and many other examples of Greek literature have survived until today.

▲ The actors in comedies wore padded costumes to make them look funny.

Drama

Drama developed from songs and dances that honored the gods. Plays were an important part of religious **festivals** and many of the theaters were built next to temples. There were two types of plays, tragedies and comedies. Comedies made fun of **politics**, religion, and important people. Tragedies were sad tales about gods, heroes, and legendary people.

▶ Greek actors always wore masks that showed different moods and expressions. The masks had wide mouths so that the actors' voices could be heard.

FastFact
Today, more than three million people live in Athens. Many of the ancient buildings are still standing.

At home

In ancient Greece, ordinary people lived in simple houses that were made from mud bricks. It was so easy to dig through the walls that burglars were known as wall-diggers! Each house was arranged around a courtyard with an altar in the middle. The living rooms were on the ground floor with bedrooms above.

Men and women often had separate living areas and spent most of their time apart. There were open fires in the kitchen and smoke escaped through a hole in the roof.

▼ This is the inside of a typical ancient Greek house.

kitchen

altar

living room

herm

Clothes

Men in ancient Greece wore tunics made from wool or linen. Over this, they wore a square piece of material, called a **chiton**, fastened at the shoulders and belted at the waist. In colder weather, men wore a cloak, called a **himation**, draped around them. In the **Classical period**, it was fashionable for men to have beards.

Women wore a long tunic, called a **peplos**. Wealthy people wore tunics made from decorated material, while slaves had plain 0tunics. Shoes were leather sandals or boots but many people went barefoot.

▼ A gold necklace of the kind worn by the woman in the vase painting (bottom).

bathroom

well

▶ This vase painting shows a woman getting ready for her wedding. She is wearing a peplos.

◀ Some houses had a statue of the god Hermes, called a herm, to guard the house.

Food

The ancient Greeks had a simple and healthy diet. They ate bread, cheese, vegetables, fruit, eggs, and meat. Many Greeks lived near the sea, so fish and seafood were popular. Olive oil was used for cooking, lighting, and cleaning.

The main meal was in the evening and the Greeks often held big dinner parties. They sat on couches, eating several courses and drinking a lot. After the meal, there was entertainment for the men at a **symposium**, or party.

▲ This vase painting shows a messenger of the gods bringing a gift of grain.

> **FastFact**
> As the Greek civilization expanded, the Roman **Empire** was just beginning. The city of Rome was founded in about 753 B.C.

▼ These are some examples of fruit that the ancient Greeks liked to eat.

pomegranates

figs

olives

dried dates

fresh dates

Greek sweetmeats

Between courses at a dinner party, the
Greeks ate sweetmeats—small snacks made
from dates, figs, nuts, sesame seeds, and honey.

Here are some for you to make.
Put $1/2$ cup (100g) of sesame seeds into a saucepan with
4 tablespoons (60ml) of honey. Ask an adult to
help you simmer the mixture over a low heat for
10–20 minutes, until it is a rich, golden color.
You can tell if it is ready by dropping a spoonful on to
a wet plate, letting it cool, then working it into a ball.
If it keeps its shape, it is ready. Take the pan off
the heat and stir the mixture every few minutes until it
is almost cold. Wet your hands with cold water and
roll spoonfuls of the mixture into 20–25 little balls.
Wrap each sweetmeat in wax paper.

grapes

Arts and crafts

The Greeks thought that there was a perfect shape for every object whether it was a simple clay pot or a huge **temple**. They used mathematics to try to make their art as beautiful as possible.

▲ The Greeks made elegant pots covered in patterns and paintings. Most of the pots were used every day for storing water, oil, or wine. Some of the most beautiful pots were buried with the dead.

◀ This statue is made from stone. The ancient Greeks were skilled sculptors and they made many statues from stone or bronze. The statues were detailed and lifelike with expressive faces and clothes that looked real. Many of them were painted but have lost their color over time.

► The Parthenon can still be found in Athens. It is one of the finest examples of ancient Greek architecture that is standing today. It was made from carved blocks of cream-colored marble held together with wooden pegs and metal clamps. The rows of columns are typical of ancient Greek buildings. This Classical style has been copied all over the world.

Bronze statues

Bronze statues were made using the "lost wax" method.

▼ When the clay and pegs were finally removed, a bronze statue was revealed.

First, a clay model was made and strengthened with wooden pegs. Then, the model was covered with a thin layer of wax. Next, the details of the statue, such as the face and clothes, were sculpted onto the wax.

The model was then covered with clay and heated so the wax melted and ran out. Molten bronze was poured in between the clay layers.

Language and learning

In ancient Greece, most children went to school. Boys went to school from the age of seven until they were 15, and learned reading, writing, and math, as well as music, poetry, and sports. Some Greek girls learned reading, writing, gymnastics, and music. Girls were also taught the skills that they would need to run a household.

In Sparta, boys were taught to be tough in order to prepare them for their life as soldiers. At the age of seven, they went to a strict school where they learned how to fight and use weapons. They often went hungry and had to sleep on the ground and were sometimes beaten.

▶ This ancient terra-cotta doll has jointed arms and legs.

◀ This is an ancient baby's bottle.

The Greek alphabet

Some Greek letters are similar to those we use today. You may have heard some of their names before. Can you think where the word "alphabet" came from?

Greek letter	Name	English sound
A α	alpha	a
B β	beta	b
Γ γ	gamma	g
Δ δ	delta	d
E ε	epsilon	e
Z ζ	zeta	z

Greek letter	Name	English sound
H η	eta	ey
Θ θ	theta	th
I ι	iota	i
K κ	kappa	k
Λ λ	lambda	l
M μ	mu	m

Greek letter	Name	English sound
N ν	nu	n
Ξ ξ	xi	ks
O o	omicron	o
Π π	pi	p
P ρ	rho	r
Σ σ,ς	sigma	s

Greek letter	Name	English sound
T τ	tau	t
Y υ	upsilon	u
Φ φ	phi	ph
X χ	chi	ch
Ψ ψ	psi	ps
Ω ω	omega	oh

The Legend of the Minotaur

The ancient Greeks told myths about their gods and about the world around them.
Myths often included real events from Greek history. This myth is about an early
civilization on the island of Crete long before Athens was a powerful city-state.
It tells the story of Theseus, a heroic young man who overcame the
Minotaur, a terrifying beast that was half-man and half-bull.

Athenians were afraid of the island of Crete and trembled at the mention of it. Every nine years, King Minos of Crete demanded a terrible tribute from the Athenians. Seven young men and seven young women were taken from Athens to be fed to the fearsome Minotaur.

King Minos would send a ship with black sails to Athens when the tribute was due. A huge crowd would gather at the harbor, weeping and wailing as the ship sailed away towards Crete.

When the prisoners arrived in Crete, they were given fine clothes and made guests of honor at a huge banquet. They were offered the most delicious food available, but they could hardly eat. Afterward, they were shut in a luxurious room, but few of them could sleep.

The next day, they were taken to some huge, wooden doors, carved with pictures of galloping bulls. From behind the doors came the sounds of loud bellowing and stamping. The prisoners were very afraid.

Then, a guard opened the doors and pushed a prisoner through. The small crowd of prisoners, guards, and priestesses outside heard a blood-curdling scream. A priestess pointed at the next prisoner to be sent through. This went on until all the prisoners had met their fate. Afterward, the Athenians rested easily for nine years, until it was time to make another tribute.

Nine years passed and the dreaded ship was sent to Athens again. Among the prisoners sent to Crete this time was a young man named Theseus. Unlike all the other prisoners, he sat dry-eyed on the ship. He laughed and chatted as they prepared for the banquet, which cheered up the other prisoners. At the banquet, Theseus sat next to King Minos' daughter, Ariadne, who was charmed by his courage and handsome looks.

Ariadne told Theseus that behind the doors there was an elaborate maze. The paths twisted and turned confusing the eye and the mind. No one who had entered the maze had ever returned.

The Minotaur lived at the heart of the maze. He knew all the twists, turns, and blind alleys. If someone stumbled into the maze, the Minotaur could find him or her in moments.

Ariadne was determined to help Theseus. After the banquet, she crept into the sleeping chamber and called softly to him. All of Theseus' weapons had been taken away, so Ariadne handed him a sword. Then she led the way to the great carved wooden doors of the maze.

"I will wait here for you," she said and handed Theseus a ball of thread.

"What is this for?" Theseus said, puzzled. "As you walk through the maze, unwind this thread behind you. If you succeed, you can follow the thread back. The Minotaur will be asleep, so creep silently through the passages until you reach his lair. With surprise on your side, you may beat him," Ariadne replied.

Theseus took the thread from Ariadne and pushed open the great door. He stepped inside and closed the door, trapping the end of the thread in it. Then, holding his sword in front of him, Theseus headed into the maze.

Theseus could hear the Minotaur snoring and he headed towards the noise. But a few minutes later, he could no longer hear the snores. The path had doubled back, and Theseus was further away from the center of the maze than when he had started. Theseus picked up the thread and followed it back to the last place where he had chosen a path.

"If I take the path that leads to the sounds, I end up farther away," he said to himself. "Perhaps if I choose the path that seems to lead away, I will get closer to him."

Theseus crept quietly along and soon found himself stumbling into the mouth of a dark cave. From inside, he heard a huge roar followed by the sound of heavy footsteps. The Minotaur had woken up! Theseus gasped and dropped his sword.

The Minotaur was even more terrifying than he had imagined. It had the body of a huge man and the head of an angry bull. Just as the Minotaur leaped forward to grab him, Theseus picked up his sword and struck the Minotaur a terrible blow on the leg.

The Minotaur was in agony. He was not used to people fighting back—his victims were usually prisoners who did not resist. Theseus struck once more with his sword. The Minotaur was caught off guard—in a moment he lay dead at Theseus' feet!

Picking up the end of the thread, brave Theseus retraced his steps through the maze. Ariadne was waiting for him at the outer doors.

Theseus was proclaimed a hero by the people of Athens. They were overjoyed that Athens no longer had to pay such a terrible tribute to King Minos of Crete.

How we know

How do we know so much about the Greeks when they lived so long ago?

Evidence from the ground

The Greeks built many buildings and made many beautiful objects. Some of these were buried and **archaeologists** have been able to dig them up to learn from them. Pictures on pottery, for example, tell us about the way that people looked.

▲ The painting on this plate shows two Greek heroes fighting over the body of a soldier.

▲ This picture is from Roman times. It shows Alexander the Great, a famous Greek military leader, going into battle against the Persian Empire.

Evidence from around us

Greek buildings that remain standing today give us evidence of how the ancient Greeks lived. And some Greek words have become part of other European languages— especially words connected with science, such as "psychology" and "astronomy."

Evidence from books

The ancient Greeks were one of the first groups of people to keep written records. They wrote down all sorts of things, from **history** and **philosophy**, to lists of goods in stores. Some of these records have survived until today. They give us important clues about the ancient Greek way of life.

▲ Theseus' temple still stands in Athens.

Glossary

Acropolis The hill within the boundary of a city-state that was used for defense. This is a Greek word, meaning "high city."

agora An open area in the center of ancient Greek cities where markets took place.

Alexander the Great The king of Macedonia and Greece who conquered the Persian Empire.

allies United territories.

archaeologist Someone who studies human history by uncovering ancient objects and physical remains.

Archaic period A period in history around 800–479 B.C.

Ariadne Daughter of King Minos who helped Theseus.

Aristotle A famous Greek philosopher and student of Plato. Aristotle died in 322 B.C.

armor A covering, usually of metal, worn to protect the body when fighting.

B.C. Before Christ; the number of years before the year zero in the Western calendar.

bronze A metal that is made of copper, tin, zinc, and lead.

Bronze Age A period in history around 3000–1000 B.C.

chiton A garment Greek men wore fastened at the shoulders and belted around the waist.

citizen In ancient Greece, a citizen was a man who had the right to own property and take part in politics and the law.

city-state An area of land around a Greek city, which had its own government but was considered a part of Greece. There were many city-states in ancient Greece.

Classical period A period in history around 479–323 B.C.

column A tall pillar, usually round, often supporting an arch or roof.

Dark Age A period in Greek history around 1000–800 B.C.

democracy A political system whereby citizens can vote for their chosen leaders and in doing so can influence decisions about the way their city or country is run.

dynasty A family that rules a country or empire for many generations.

empire A large group of states or countries ruled by a single government, usually an emperor.

epic A long, traditional poem that tells a story about heroes or the gods.

festival A special day, or several days, of celebration.

Helen of Troy Wife of the king of Sparta, Menelaus, and cause of the Trojan War.

Hellenistic Age A period in Greek history around 323–31 B.C.

himation A type of cloak worn by Greek men.

history The study of important or public events from the past.

Homer An ancient Greek storyteller. Homer wrote two famous epic poems about the Trojan War. They are called *The Iliad* and *The Odyssey*.

knucklebones The bones from the ankles of animals.

such as pigs and goats that were thrown into the air like dice.

logic A method of thinking a problem through carefully to find a solution.

Menelaus The king of Sparta, married to Helen of Troy.

Minos The king of Crete.

Minotaur A beast in Greek mythology who was half-man and half-bull. The Minotaur lived at the center of a huge maze on the island of Crete.

monarchy A country that has a monarchy is ruled by a king or queen. Usually, when the king or queen dies, their son or daughter becomes the next ruler.

Mount Olympus The mountain in Greece where the gods were thought to live.

myths Traditional stories about gods or heroes. Greek mythology continues to influence writers today.

oracle A holy place where priests and priestesses asked the gods for advice.

ostrakon A pottery fragment that citizens wrote on to vote against a politician.

peplos A long tunic worn by women in ancient Greece.

philosopher A person who studies the world around them. This word comes from the Greek words for "lover of wisdom."

Plato A Greek philosopher who died in 347 B.C.

politics This word, which comes from the Greek word, *politikos*, refers to the management of a country or state. A country's "political system" is its rules of government.

priest A man who devotes his life to serving a god or gods.

priestess A woman who devotes her life to serving a god or gods.

sacrifice An offering, usually of an animal, made to the gods asking them to bring good fortune to people.

sculpture Art in a solid form, such as a statue or carving. Sculpture was highly prized in ancient Greece.

slave A worker who was legally owned by a citizen in ancient Greece and had no rights at all. Slavery is now illegal in all countries.

Socrates One of the first Greek philosophers, Socrates lived in Athens from around 469 to 399 B.C.

soothsayer A person who could predict the future and tell fortunes.

statue A model of a person, an animal, or a god. Greek sculptors made many statues.

symposium A party, attended by ancient Greek men, where entertainment took place.

temple A building for the worship of a god or goddess, or that is thought of as his or her home.

terra-cotta Brownish-red pottery used in building and modeling. The word comes from the Italian words for "baked earth."

Theseus A hero in Greek mythology who killed the Minotaur and ended the Athenians' nine-yearly human sacrifice to Crete.

tribute A gift that is given to show respect for someone.

triremes The biggest ships in the Athenian fleet. They were about 130ft (40m) long and could reach speeds of up to 10mph (16km/h).

Workbook

Photocopy this sheet and use it to make your own notes.

Workbook

Draw your own Greek city

Questions and answers

The Pythia was the **priestess** at the **oracle** in Delphi in ancient Greece. She was very wise and people often went to ask her questions. She can answer all your questions about ancient Greek civilization.

What did the Greeks discover about math and science?

The ancient Greeks made many important discoveries in mathematics and science. For example, the scientist Democritus developed a theory that everything on Earth was made up of tiny particles called atoms. This theory has been a key part of science since this important discovery.

The temple of the priest Trophonius was unusual in that only men were allowed to speak the words of the oracle. The cave in which Trophonius' oracle was found was said to be so awe-inspiring that people who entered and consulted the oracle never smiled again!

Priest

What did the Greeks discover about medicine?

Many people believed that illness was actually a punishment from the gods. But a **philosopher** named Hippocrates developed a scientific approach to medicine. He carefully studied the human body and performed experiments to discover the real causes of illness. Sometimes, Hippocrates is called the "Father of Medicine."

What was life like for women in ancient Greece?

Women in ancient Greece were not allowed to vote. They could go out to religious **festivals** or to visit friends, but they were expected to be accompanied by a friend or a **slave**. Women organized the household and the slaves, and spinning and weaving took up a lot of their time.

What was life like for children in ancient Greece?

At about seven years old, children began to learn reading, writing, poetry, mathematics, and music. But Greek children also played with dolls, rattles, dice or **knucklebones**, and even yo-yos.

How did the Greeks travel?

Wealthy people owned horses. Some merchants used carts, drawn by oxen or mules, to transport their goods. Most Greeks traveled on foot. Many people of the **city-states** traveled in ships to trade.

What is a democracy?

A democracy is a system of government in which the leaders are chosen by the people. In ancient Greece, many of the city-states were governed by a democracy. **Citizens** were able to vote, and could also become politicians and serve as members on juries in the law courts.

Who was Socrates?

Socrates was a philosopher who was sentenced to death by the citizens of Athens. They thought that he was a bad influence on young people and that he had tried to introduce new gods. Socrates' teachings and the story of his death were written down by another Greek philosopher, **Plato**.

What did the Greeks do in their spare time?

Most of the entertainment was based on religion. There were drama, poetry, and music festivals to honor the gods. During the drama festivals, businesses closed and prisoners were allowed out of jail! Poetry was recited at festivals and private parties and often accompanied by music.

What is a marathon?

Marathon was a town in ancient Greece northeast of Athens. In 490 B.C., the Persians landed here to attack the Athenians. An Athenian messenger was sent to Sparta to ask for help—and he ran all the way. That's about 150 miles (240km)! And that's why a long running race is called a marathon!

In ancient Greece, priestesses had a much easier life than other women. Other women had hard housework to do. The Pythia at Delphi was the priestess of Apollo. She got her inspiration for oracles by inhaling gases coming up from a hole in the ground while sitting over it on a three-legged stool!

Priestess

Why were sports and athletics so important to the Greeks?

The Greeks believed that having a fit body was a way of honoring the gods and they used sport as a way of training for warfare. Men's events included running, wrestling, boxing, and javelin-throwing. In all of these events, the athletes competed naked! Women competed in running races. Greeks took the games very seriously, and breaking the rules in sport was punished severely.

FastFact
The Persian **Empire** was also expanding around 550 B.C. The Persians become powerful at this time under the rule of a man named Cyrus the Great.

Index

www.two-canpublishing.com

Published by Two-Can Publishing
234 Nassau Street, Princeton, NJ 08542

Copyright © 2001, Two-Can Publishing

For information on Two-Can books and multimedia, call
1-609-921-6700, fax 1-609-921-3349, or visit our Web site.

'Two-Can' is a trademark of Two-Can Publishing.
Two-Can Publishing is a division of Zenith Entertainment Ltd,
43–45 Dorset Street, London W1U 7NA.

ISBN 1-58728-760-9

1 2 3 4 5 6 7 8 9 10 03 02 01

Photograph credits: AKG Photo: front cover;
Ancient Art and Architecture Collection: p.11 (r), p.14,
p.15 (b), p.20, p.23 (t); Bridgeman Art Library: p.26 (r),
p.27 (b); ET Archive: p.17, p.34 (l); Werner Forman:
pp.6–7; Michael Holford: p.11 (t,c), p.15 (t), p.19,
p.23 (b), p.24 (t), p.26 (l), p.27 (t), p.28, p.34 (tr), p.46,
p.47; Toby Maudsley: pp.25–25 (b), Zefa: p.34 (br).
Illustration credits: Mike Allport: pp.4–27, p.47, p.48;
Maxine Hamil: pp.29–33; Michele Egar, Carlo Tartaglia and
Jon Stuart: pp.8–9, pp.12–13, pp.44–45.

Every effort has been made to acknowledge correctly and
contact the source of each picture and Two-Can Publishing
apologises for any unintentional errors or omissions which
will be corrected in future editions of this book.

Printed in Hong Kong by Wing King Tong

This title previously published in a large format.